Note to Parents and Teachers

The SCIENCE STARTERS series introduces key science vocabulary and concepts to young children while encouraging them to discover and understand the world around them. The series works as a set of graded readers in three levels.

LEVEL 3: READ ALONE
These books can be read alone or as part of guided or group reading. Each book has three sections:

- Information pages that introduce key concepts. Key words appear in bold for easy recognition on pages where the related science concepts are explained.
- A lively story that recalls this vocabulary and encourages children to use these words when they talk and write.
- A quiz asks children to look back and recall what they have read.

WHERE WILDLIFE LIVES looks at HABITATS. Below are some answers and activities related to the questions on the information spreads that parents, carers, and teachers can use to discuss and develop further ideas and concepts:

p. 6 *Where would you find a woodlouse, worm, snail, butterfly, or frog?* Woodlice are found under logs, worms in the soil, snails in damp places, butterflies near flowers, and frogs in a pond.

p. 9 *Can you think of any other predators and the prey that they eat?* Ask children to think about predators and prey in different habitats, e.g. shark and fish in the ocean, blackbird and worm in garden, or polar bear and seal in the Arctic.

p. 11 *What other animals have adapted to life in towns?* e.g. squirrels and pigeons. Ask children how animals have adapted to life in other habitats, e.g. deserts or the Arctic.

p. 13 *What other sounds might you hear in a wood or forest?* e.g. birdsong, rustling in leaves. Ask about sounds you might hear in other habitats, e.g. seashore, river, meadow.

p. 15 *Why should they be careful not to touch insects?* Some insects can give a painful sting or bite. You could also warn children about other animals that sting or bite, e.g. jellyfish, crabs, spiders, prickly sea urchins, as well as stinging plants such as nettles.

p. 17 *What might she find (in pond or river water)?* Insects such as whirligigs and water boatmen, water snails, mosquito larvae, frogspawn, and water plants.

p. 19 *When is a good time to look for seashells?* When the tide is out.

p. 21 *What other animals can you find inside your home?* Look out for flying insects such as flies and wasps, creepy crawlies such as ants, and birds nesting in the roof.

ADVISORY TEAM

Educational Consultant
Andrea Bright—Science Coordinator, Trafalgar Junior School

Literacy Consultant
Jackie Holderness—former Senior Lecturer in Primary Education, Westminster Institute, Oxford Brookes University

Series Consultants
Anne Fussell—Early Years Teacher and University Tutor, Westminster Institute, Oxford Brookes University

David Fussell—C.Chem., FRSC

CONTENTS

4	Habitats
6	Living Things
8	Food Chains
10	Exploring Habitats
12	Trees and Woods
14	Meadows
16	Ponds and Rivers
18	The Seashore
20	Town Wildlife
22	Habitats in Danger
24	**Story: Seaside Explorers** James and Dan discover some amazing animals on the beach.
31	Quiz
32	Index

© Aladdin Books Ltd 2006

Designed and produced by
Aladdin Books Ltd

First published in
the United States in 2006 by
Stargazer Books
c/o The Creative Company
123 South Broad Street
P.O. Box 227, Mankato,
Minnesota 56002

Printed in Malaysia
All rights reserved

Editor: Sally Hewitt
Design: Flick, Book Design and Graphics

Thanks to:
• Ciannait O'Donnell, Georgia Jedwab, and Hugh and Luke Pullman for appearing as models in this book, and to Ronan O'Donnell and Rob Pullman for helping to organize the photoshoots.
• The pupils and teachers of Trafalgar Junior School and St. Nicholas C.E. Infant School for testing the sample books.

Library of Congress Cataloging-in-Publication Data

Pipe, Jim, 1966-
  Habitats / by Jim Pipe.
    p. cm. -- (Science starters. Level 3)
  ISBN 1-59604-013-0
  1. Habitat (Ecology)--Juvenile literature.
  I. Title. II. Series

QH541.14.P57 2005
577--dc22
                                  2005042654

Photocredits:
l-left, r-right, b-bottom, t-top, c-center, m-middle
Cover tl, 17br — Ronan O'Donnell. Cover tr, 11br, 16m, 20tr, 21t, 29br — Flick Smith. Cover tm — Otto Rogge Photography. Cover main — Comstock. 4tl, 21br, 31bl — Digital Vision. 4b, 5t, 6mc, 8b, 9tc, 13bl, 31tr, 31ml, 31brc — Corbis. 5m, 15tr, 23t, 31mr — TongRo. 5b — Marc Arundale/ Select Pictures. 6br, 7 both, 9tr, 24br, 28bl — Stockbyte. 8tl, 11mr, 13tl, 25tl, 30mr — John Foxx Images. 9tl, 21bl, 23br — USDA. 9bl — US Fish & Wildlife. 9br, 26br — Ingram Publishing. 10tr, 24l, 25br, 26tr & ml, 27br, 28-29m both — Jim Pipe. 10b, 11ml, 14br, 16br, 22tr, 24tr — Digital Vision. 12b, 16m, 20b — US Fish & Wildlife. 13mr, 19t — Corel. 18l — EU archive. 21ml & bl — Photodisc.

SCIENCE STARTERS
LEVEL 3

HABITATS

Where Wildlife Lives

by Jim Pipe

Stargazer Books

HABITATS

A home is a place where we can eat, drink, sleep, work, and play.

Animals and plants need homes too. They need a place where there is food, water, shelter, and space to live in.

This place is called a **habitat**.

Mountain habitat

Habitats can be big or small. They can be wet or dry, hot or cold, bright or dark.

Some habitats are huge areas like deserts, mountains, or the ocean.

Local habitats are woods, ponds, rivers, meadows, and the seashore.

Small places like a patch of grass or a windowbox are habitats too.

LIVING THINGS

All **living things** need a habitat to live in.

Plants and animals usually share a habitat with other **living things**.

Look at this woodland scene. What **living things** can you see?

Not all living things are plants or animals.

Mushrooms are living things called fungi.

Wood

Butterfly in the air

Where would you expect to find a woodlouse, worm, snail, butterfly, or frog?

All sorts of **living things** share the same habitat. They use the habitat in different ways.

In a river, some plants grow underwater. Trees and bushes live on the riverbank.

Fish live underwater, but birds and insects live on it.

Deer and mice live on land near the river.

Birds on the water

Fish underwater

FOOD CHAINS

A habitat provides living things with food and water.

Plants make food from sunlight and from minerals in the soil. Plants are food for many animals from caterpillars to elephants!

Zebras eat grass

Lions eat zebras

Plant-eating animals are often eaten by other animals, called predators.
The animals that predators eat are their prey.

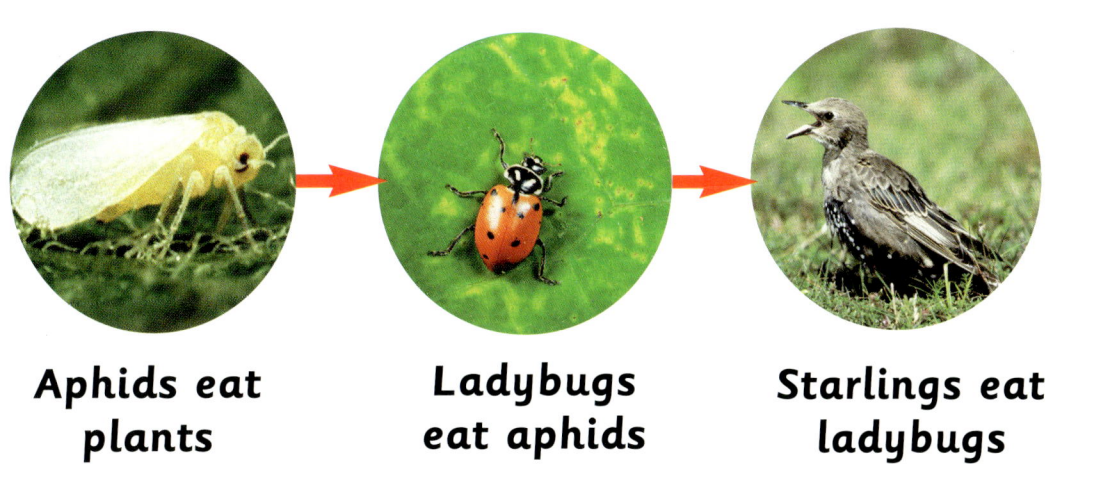

Aphids eat plants   **Ladybugs eat aphids**   **Starlings eat ladybugs**

A **food chain** shows what living things eat in a habitat. The arrows go from one living thing to the living thing that eats it.

Can you draw a **food chain** showing that zebras eat grass and lions eat zebras?

Rabbit

Fox

Look at this pair of animals. The fox is the predator and the rabbit is its prey.

Can you think of any other predators and the prey that they eat?

EXPLORING HABITATS

We share habitats with other animals and plants. If you want to **explore** a habitat, remember that it is their home too.

Try to watch animals without disturbing them. If you touch pond water or soil, remember to wash your hands afterward.

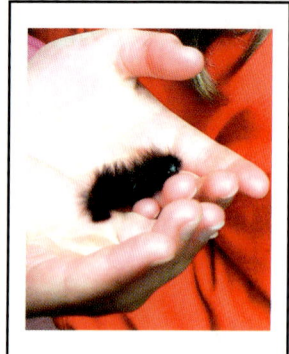

If you move an animal, return it to the place where you found it.

Take care near water

Always take an adult when you go **exploring**.

Most kinds of plant and animal have lived in the same habitat for thousands of years. Their body suits the habitat they live in.

If we damage a habitat, the animals in it may not be able to live anywhere else.

This dolphin can't live in a forest.

This gibbon can't live in the ocean.

Kestrel

Some kestrels hunt in towns and cities. They have changed, or adapted, to a new habitat.

What other animals have adapted to life in towns?

11

TREES AND WOODS

One **tree** can be a habitat for thousands of living things.

Centipedes hunt slugs and worms in the rotting leaves at the base of a **tree**.

Weevils and beetles feed on **tree** bark. Bugs and caterpillars nibble new leaves.

Weevil

Tree

Trees grow together to form **woods** and forests, a habitat for all kinds of animals.

Birds and squirrels make their nests in **trees**.
They eat nuts, berries, and the minibeasts that live on **trees**.

Squirrel   **Deer**

Larger animals such as deer and badgers live on the forest floor.

Woodpecker

Forest animals are hard to see. But you can listen for the noises they make. Woodpeckers looking for insects tap on tree trunks.

What other sounds might you hear in a wood or forest?

MEADOWS

When a field is left uncut it grows into a **meadow** of tall grasses and wildflowers.

Many flowers live in a **meadow**, such as thistles, buttercups, poppies, and foxgloves.

Their bright colors attract insects such as bees, wasps, and butterflies.

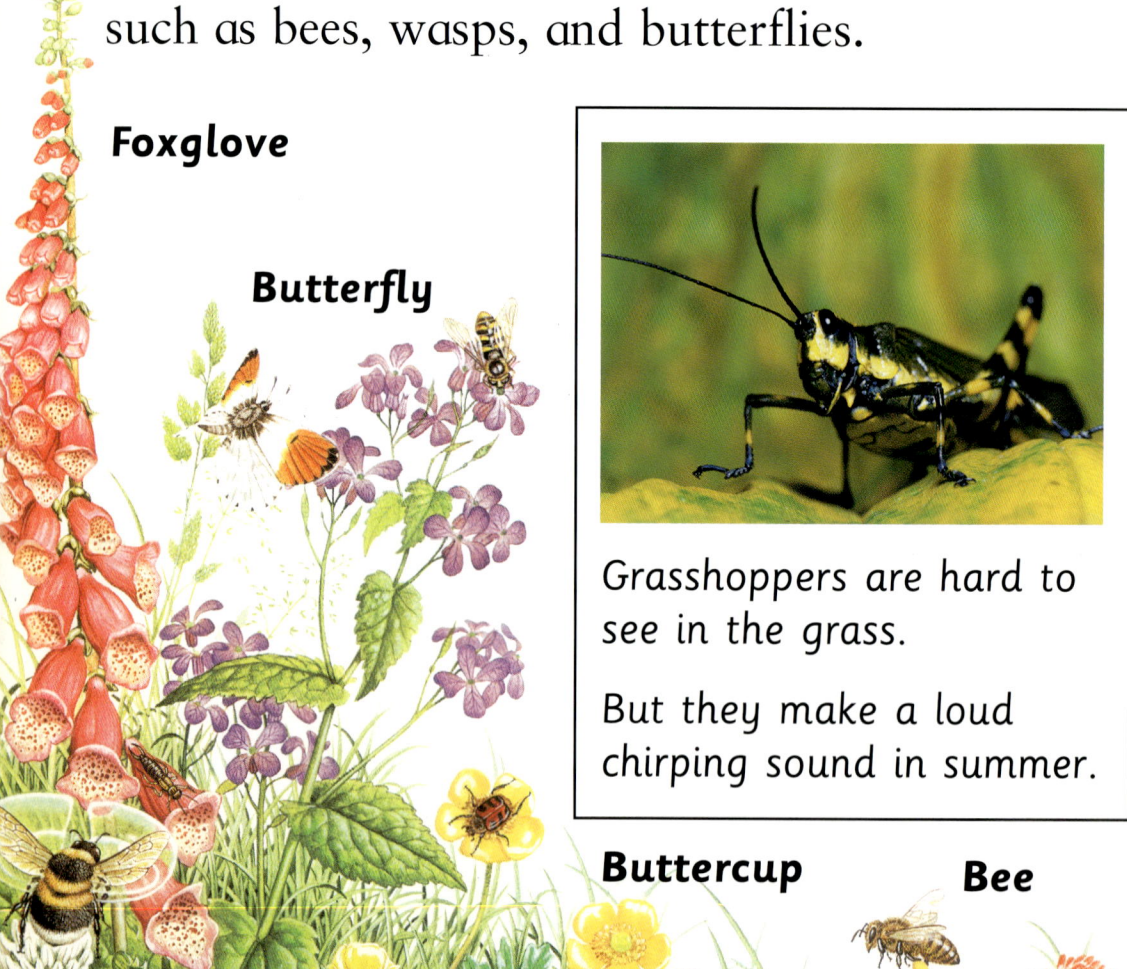

Foxglove

Butterfly

Grasshoppers are hard to see in the grass.

But they make a loud chirping sound in summer.

Buttercup

Bee

14

These children are catching insects in a net.

Why should they be careful not to touch the insects?

Birds such as skylarks and blackbirds visit **meadows** to eat seeds, worms, and insects.

Mammals such as mice and rabbits make their homes in holes underground.

Foxes and owls hunt them at night.

Blackbird

Blackberries

Thistles

PONDS AND RIVERS

Many animals live in and around **ponds** and **rivers**. Insects, turtles, and fish feed on plants that live underwater.

Dragonfly

Insects such as whirligigs and pond skaters live on the surface of the water.

Dragonflies and frogs hunt flies that live in the air above a **pond**.

Frog

Whirligig

Unlike a **pond**, the water in a **river** is always moving.

Ducks and swans live on the water. They eat plants and insects. They build nests on the riverbank.

Kingfisher

Kingfishers and otters live on riverbanks. They hunt for fish under the water.

Otters

This girl is pond dipping. She uses a jelly jar to collect water from a river.

She uses a magnifying glass to see small animals in the water. What might she find?

THE SEASHORE

The **seashore** is home to many unusual plants and animals.

On a sandy beach, clams and other shellfish bury themselves in the sand.

Clam

Beach

Crabs scuttle across the beach, using their large claws to grab prey.

Higher up the beach, long grasses live in the sand dunes.

Seaweed

Starfish

The sea moves up and down the beach twice a day. This is called the tide.

When is a good time to look for seashells?

On a rocky beach, pools are left behind when the tide goes out. Plants called seaweed cling to rocks.

Limpets feed on the seaweed and in turn are prey for starfish. Small fish and crabs hunt shrimp hiding in the seaweed.

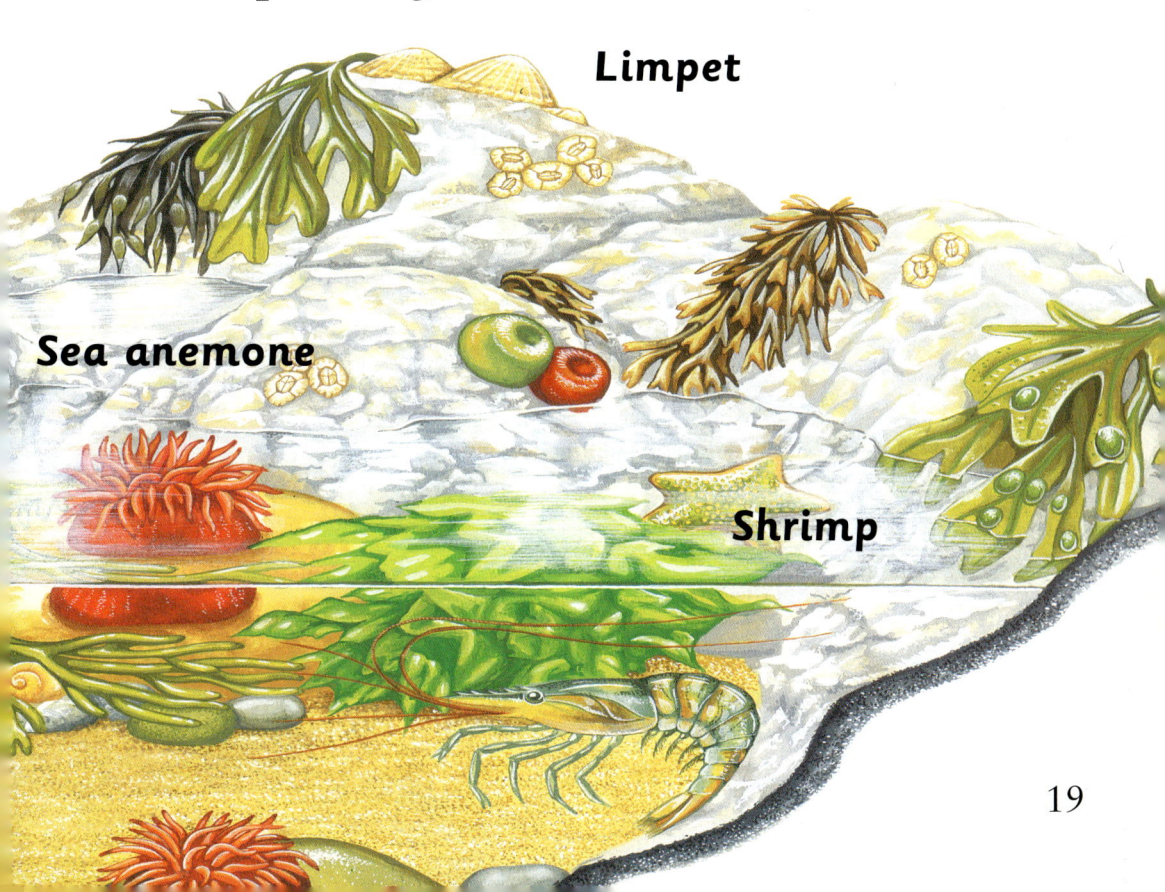

Limpet

Sea anemone

Shrimp

TOWN WILDLIFE

Many animals have learned to live in a **town** or city habitat.

The trees and bushes in parks provide food and shelter for insects, birds, squirrels, and even deer.

At night, foxes hunt for food in city trashcans.

Town pond

We can help town wildlife by leaving out food.

We can plant flowers that attract insects.

Town houses are a habitat for all sorts of birds. Pigeons nest on high buildings. Sparrows nest under roofs.

Mice and rats can live inside walls or under floors.

Minibeasts such as moths, cockroaches, ants, and beetles can live inside your house.

Some animals live on us, such as fleas, nits, and ticks!

Tick

Some animals help to keep our home clean. Spiders eat flies which spread germs.

What other animals can you find inside your home?

Spider

HABITATS IN DANGER

Some habitats are in **danger**. When people cut down forests or turn meadows into farms, they kill wild plants.

They also destroy animal homes. Some animals die straight away. Others try to move to a new home.

The new home may not have enough food and shelter for extra animals.

Cutting down trees

We also damage habitats and wildlife when we pollute them with oil or chemicals.

Pollution

Meadow

We can also create new habitats. We can let an area of grass grow long to create a meadow.

We can plant a tree. One day it will be a home to lots of animals. We can build a pond to make a home for water creatures.

Digging a pond

Look around your school or home. How could you make new habitats for animals to live in?

THE STORY

SEASIDE EXPLORER

Look for words and ideas about habitats and living things.

It was a lovely spring day. Dan and James were feeling bored in the house, so Dad took them to the beach.

"It's a bit cold to go swimming," said Dan.
"Yes, but look at all that sand," said James.
"Let's go exploring!"

"A beach is a home for lots of living things," said Dad "Let's see how many we can find."

"There are lots of different places to look," said Dan. "On the way here I saw seagulls on the cliffs."

"I hope we see dolphins," said James. "Let's climb up to the sand dunes. We can see far out to sea from there."

"I can see some animals," said Dan. "That family is having a picnic in the long grass!"

"Do you think they're wild?" joked James.

The boys looked for rabbits in the dunes. "They may be hiding underground in their burrows," said Dad. "Lots of predators like to eat rabbits!"

"I've found a paw print!" shouted James.

"It looks like a dog's paw," said Dan. "I saw a woman walking her dog along the beach!"

25

The boys walked toward the water. Below the dunes was a line of seaweed and shells. "Look how far the tide comes in," said Dan.

"What's this long shell?" asked James. "It's a razor shell," said Dad. "It's from a razor clam, an animal that burrows into the sand."

Farther along the beach, Dan found a starfish. "I hope the tide comes in soon and washes it back to sea."

The boys explored the beach for two more hours. But they found only shells and seaweed.

"Don't worry," said Dad. "I know a rocky beach we can go to tomorrow."

The next day, Dan spotted some familiar faces when they arrived at the rocky beach.
"It's that family from the sand dunes."

"The girl is collecting shells on the beach," said Dad. "Maybe she knows a good place to look for animals."

Paula lived near the beach and knew it well. She showed the boys some different types of seaweed.

Then they walked over to the rockpools.
"Watch out," said Paula.
"These rocks are very slippery."

All around the rockpool, limpets clung to the rocks.

"Some people scrape limpets off the rocks," said Paula.
"But they're food for many crabs and starfish."

Paula pointed out some sea anemones.
"They look pretty, but they are deadly predators," she said.
"They attack prey with their poison tentacles."

"There's a little fish in the rocks. Will the anemone get it?" asked Dan.

"Phew! It got away this time."

Something else was moving under the water. It was a hermit crab.

"You can pick it up if you are gentle," said Dad. "Watch out, even tiny claws can pinch!"

When he had shown the boys, Dad put the crab back where he found it. It scuttled under a big stone.

As they walked back along the beach, the children were attacked by a big swarm of flies.

"The flies lay their eggs in the seaweed," said Paula. "But they love to suck blood from bigger animals like us. Run for it!"

"Thanks for showing us the rockpools," said Dan. "You never know what you'll find," said Paula. "The seashore is a habitat for so many animals."

Suddenly, James shouted out, "Look! It's a seal!"

"Is that his home?" asked Dan. "Kind of," said Paula. "His home stretches all around the world—it's the ocean!"

> **WRITE YOUR OWN STORY** about exploring a habitat. You also could do a drawing of a habitat showing where different animals and plants live, like this picture of a beach.
>
> Seagulls
> Rabbits
> Crabs
> Seaweed
> Razor shells
> Fish
> Limpets
> Starfish
> Seals

QUIZ

Are all living things plants or animals?

Answer on pages 6

What does a lion eat?
Is a lion a predator or prey?

Answer on page 8

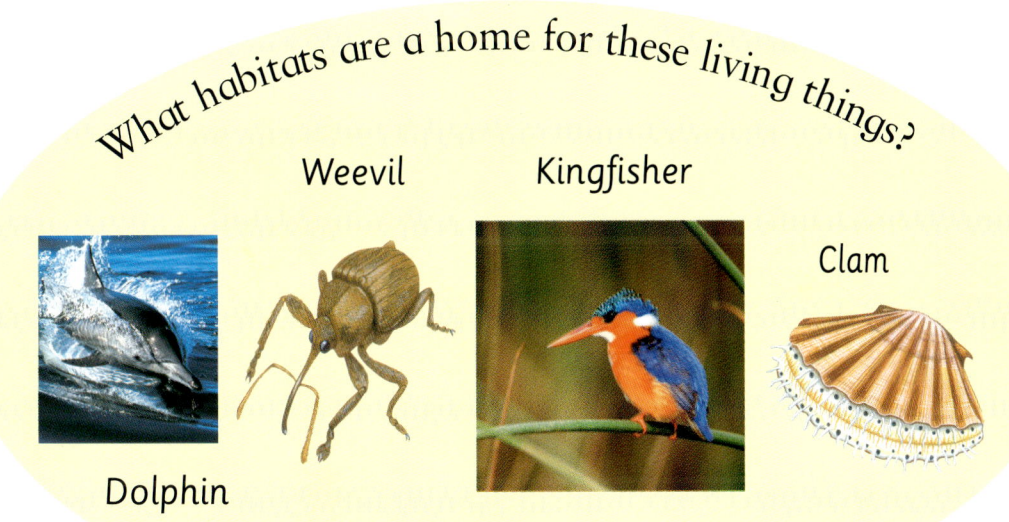

How can we create new habitats?

Answer on page 23

What habitats are a home for these living things?

Weevil

Kingfisher

Clam

Dolphin

Answers on pages 13, 15, 27, 28

31

INDEX

aphids 9

beaches 21, 24
blackberries 15
blackbirds 15
buttercups 14
butterflies 6, 14

clams 18, 26
crabs 29

deer 13
deserts 5
dipping 17
dolphins 11, 25
dragonflies 16

exploring 10

fish 7
flowers 14
food chains 9
foxes 9, 20
foxgloves 14
frogs 16

gibbons 11
grass 8
grasshoppers 14

habitats 4, 5
 in danger 22, 23
homes 4

kestrels 11
kingfishers 17

ladybugs 9
limpets 19, 28
lions 8
living things 6, 7

meadows 14, 15, 23
mice 7, 15
mountains 5
mushrooms 6

otters 17

pigeons 21
ponds 16, 17, 20

rabbits 9
razor shells 26, 30
rivers 5, 7, 10, 16, 17

rockpools 19, 27, 28, 29

sea anemones 19, 28
seashore 18, 19
seaweed 18, 27
shells 19
shrimp 19
spiders 21
squirrels 13, 2
starfish 18, 26
starlings 9

ticks 21
town wildlife 20, 21
trees 7, 12, 13, 22

wasps 14
weevils 12
whirligigs 16
windowboxes
woodpeckers 1
woods 6, 13

zebra 8

32